D0773579

WITHDRAWN

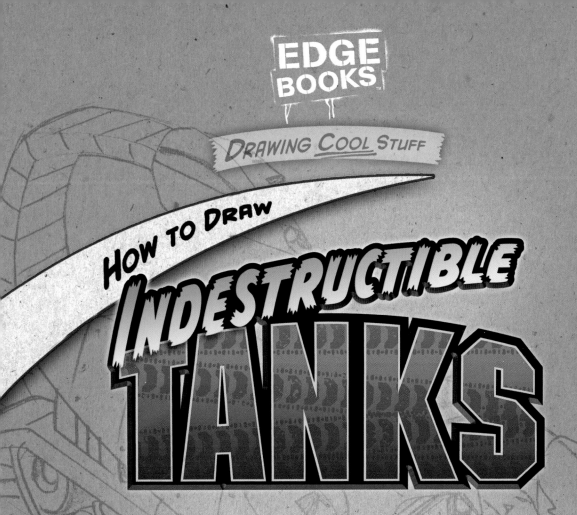

EDGE BOOKS™

DRAWING COOL STUFF

HOW TO DRAW

INDESTRUCTIBLE TANKS

by Aaron Sautter

illustrated by Rod Whigham

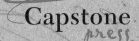

Capstone
press®

Mankato, Minnesota

Edge Books are published by Capstone Press,
151 Good Counsel Drive, P.O. Box 669, Mankato, Minnesota 56002.
www.capstonepub.com

Copyright © 2008 by Capstone Press, a Capstone imprint.
All rights reserved. No part of this publication may be reproduced in whole
or in part, or stored in a retrieval system, or transmitted in any form or by any
means, electronic, mechanical, photocopying, recording, or otherwise, without
written permission of the publisher.
For information regarding permission, write to Capstone Press,
151 Good Counsel Drive, P.O. Box 669, Dept. R, Mankato, Minnesota 56002.
Printed in the United States of America in Stevens Point, Wisconsin.

052010
005790R

Library of Congress Cataloging-in-Publication Data
Sautter, Aaron.
    How to draw indestructible tanks / by Aaron Sautter; illustrated by Rod Whigham.
    p. cm. — (Edge books. Drawing cool stuff)
    Includes bibliographical references and index.
    Summary: "Lively text and fun illustrations describe how to draw indestructible
tanks" — Provided by publisher.
    ISBN–13: 978-1-4296-1301-9 (hardcover)
    ISBN–10: 1-4296-1301-7 (hardcover)
    1. Tanks (Military science) in art — Juvenile literature. 2. Drawing —
Technique — Juvenile literature. I. Whigham, Rod, 1954– II. Title. III. Series.
NC825.T36S28 2008
743'.8962374752 — dc22   2007025106

Credits
Jason Knudson, set designer; Patrick D. Dentinger, book designer

TABLE OF CONTENTS

WELCOME!

You probably picked this book because you think tanks are cool. Or you picked it because you like to draw. Whatever the reason, get ready to dive into the world of indestructible tanks!

Tanks have been unstoppable battle machines since World War I (1914-1918). They can travel over almost any terrain, and their huge guns strike fear into the hearts of opposing armies. Tanks can be many shapes and sizes, but they all have one thing in common — they are all awesome forces of destruction!

This book is just a starting point. Once you've learned how to draw the different tanks in this book, you can start drawing your own. Let your imagination run wild, and see what sorts of big, powerful tanks you can create.

To get started, you'll need some supplies:

1. First you'll need drawing paper. Any type of blank, unlined paper will do.

2. Pencils are the easiest to use for your drawing projects. Make sure you have plenty of them.

3. You have to keep your pencils sharp to make clean lines. Keep a pencil sharpener close by. You'll use it a lot.

4. As you practice drawing, you'll need a good eraser. Pencil erasers wear out very fast. Get a rubber or kneaded eraser. You'll be glad you did.

5. When your drawing is finished, you can trace over it with a black ink pen or thin felt-tip marker. The dark lines will really make your work stand out.

6. If you decide to color your drawings, colored pencils and markers usually work best. You can also use colored pencils to shade your drawings and make them more lifelike.

M4 SHERMAN

The M4 Sherman was the main tank used by the United States in World War II (1939-1945). German-built tanks were larger and more powerful, but Sherman tanks were quicker and more reliable. The United States built about 50,000 Sherman tanks during the war.

After drawing this tank, try showing it fighting in a World War II battle!

STEP 1

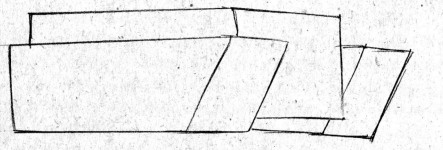

STEP 2

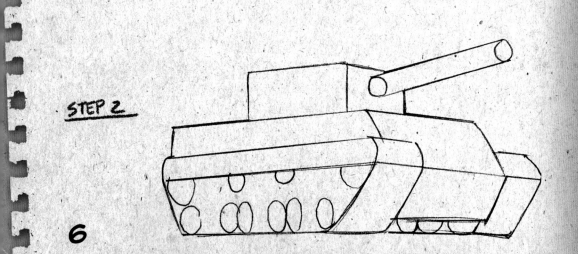

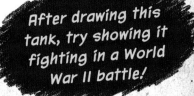

STEP 3

STEP 4

FINAL!

7

M109 PALADIN

The M109 Paladin is more of a rolling cannon than a tank. Its ammunition weighs nearly 100 pounds, and it can hit a target up to 18 miles away! No enemy is safe when these beasts rumble into battle.

After practicing this tank, try it again as it fires its huge cannon!

STEP 1

STEP 2

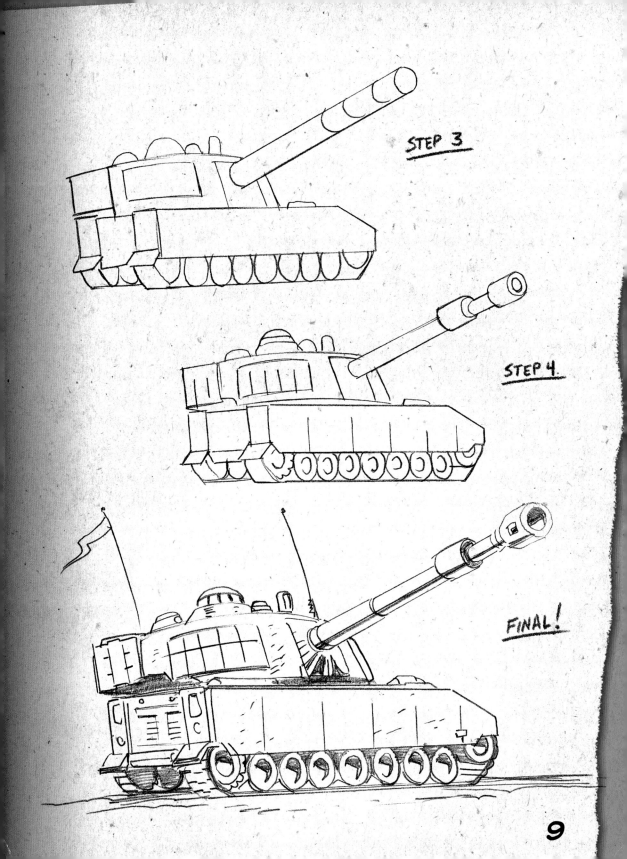

STEP 3

STEP 4

FINAL!

9

BLT BRIDGE LAYER

Marching armies don't have time to search for easy river crossings. Instead, they use the Bridge Layer Tank (BLT) to cross over difficult obstacles. Its 65-foot bridge lets soldiers and heavy war machines easily cross deep rivers and ravines.

After drawing this tank, try it again as it extends its bridge over a river!

STEP 1

STEP 2

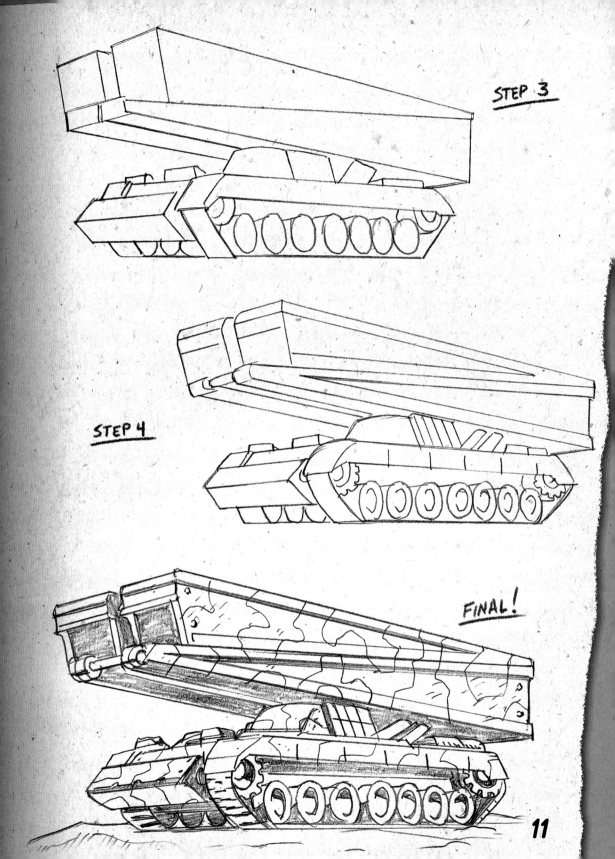

STEP 3

STEP 4

FINAL!

11

MK2 FLAME THROWER

Ground soldiers need to keep a sharp eye out for the MK2 Flame Thrower. This monster can blast targets up to 300 feet away. It's a devastating weapon in close combat. Plus, it's very useful for flushing out enemies hiding inside buildings.

After practicing this tank, try it again as it scorches a battlefield!

STEP 1

STEP 2

STEP 3

STEP 4

FINAL!

13

S7 DRIFT BUSTER

Blinding blizzards and giant snowdrifts are no match for the S7 Drift Buster. This high-tech tank is useful on all frozen terrain. No matter how slick the ice or how deep the snow, winter has no effect on this mighty war machine.

When you're done drawing this tank, try creating your own fun tank design!

STEP 1

STEP 2

STEP 3

STEP 4

FINAL!

15

AMX MINE SWEEPER

Many soldiers have been injured or killed in battle by hidden land mines. The AMX Mine Sweeper helps clear out mines in front of a marching army. It uses strong magnetic fields to set off the mines, creating a safe path for soldiers to follow.

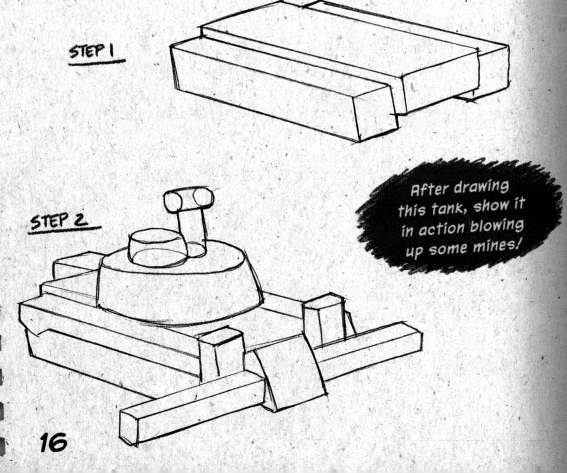

STEP 1

STEP 2

After drawing this tank, show it in action blowing up some mines!

STEP 3

STEP 4

FINAL!

17

ST2 OCEAN CRAWLER

In the future, tanks will have more uses than just fighting battles. The ST2 Ocean Crawler may be used as a research vehicle to explore the ocean floor. Its crablike arms can be used to gather rock samples or to fend off attacks from giant squid!

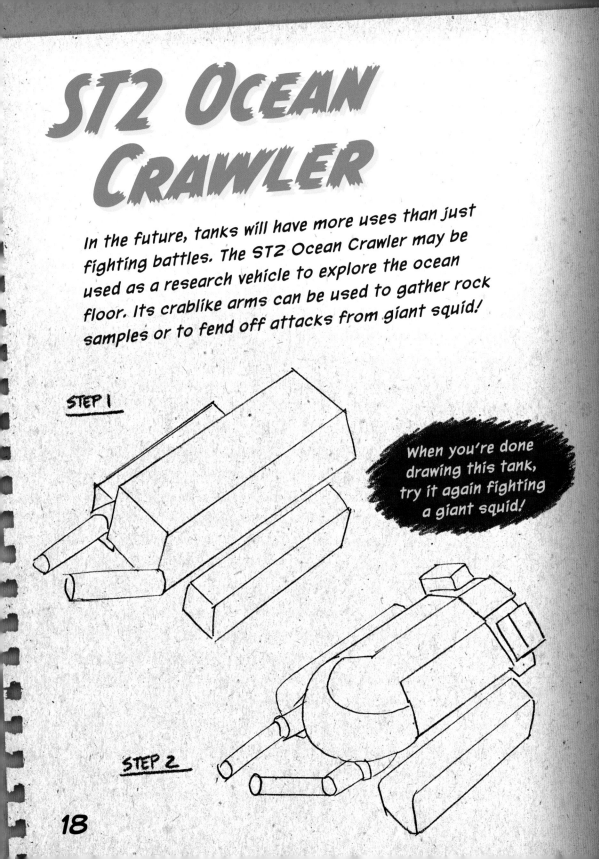

STEP 1

When you're done drawing this tank, try it again fighting a giant squid!

STEP 2

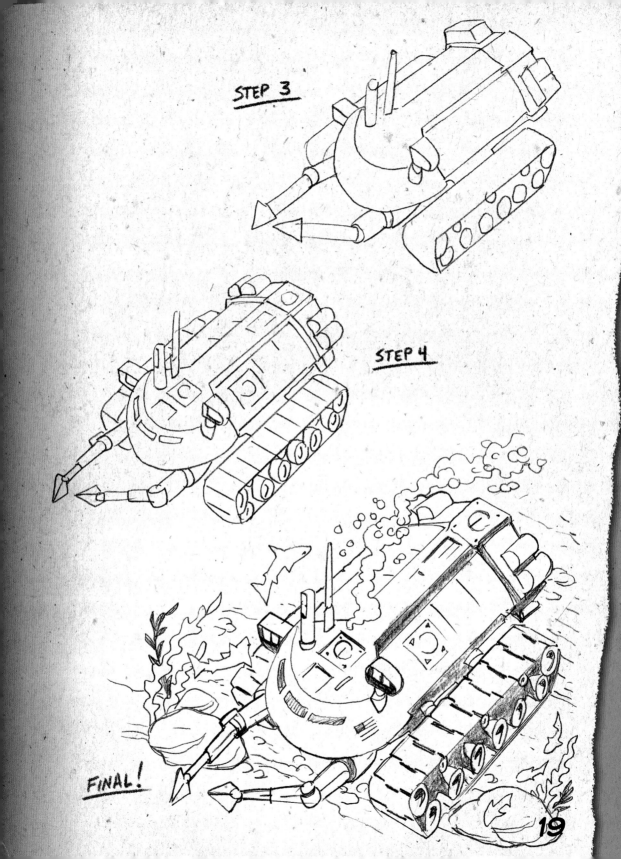

STEP 3

STEP 4

FINAL!

19

MARTIAN-MB3

The Martian-MB3 battle tank was first used during the Martian World War of 2138. It was an effective tool in ending the war. Its unique design allowed it to easily travel across the rough terrain of Mars. And its powerful laser cannon could quickly destroy enemy base camps.

After practicing this tank, try showing it rolling across the red sand dunes of Mars!

STEP 1

STEP 2

STEP 3

STEP 4

FINAL!

21

SKORP-7

The futuristic Skorp-7 is based on a scorpion's deadly features. Its two powerful pincers can rip through almost any armor. And the tail's powerful plasma cannon can blast up to 50 enemy targets per minute. Soldiers need to stay out of sight when this menace rolls into view!

After drawing this tank, try it again blasting its huge plasma cannon!

STEP 1

STEP 2

STEP 3

STEP 4

FINAL!

23

THE ANNIHILATOR

The Annihilator is a destructive war machine on the planet Zurgo-6. With its turbo-powered engines, it can zoom to a battlefield in a matter of minutes. The engines also power its huge disintegrator beam, which can destroy whole armies in seconds!

After drawing this tank, try it again as it cruises across an alien planet!

STEP 1

STEP 2

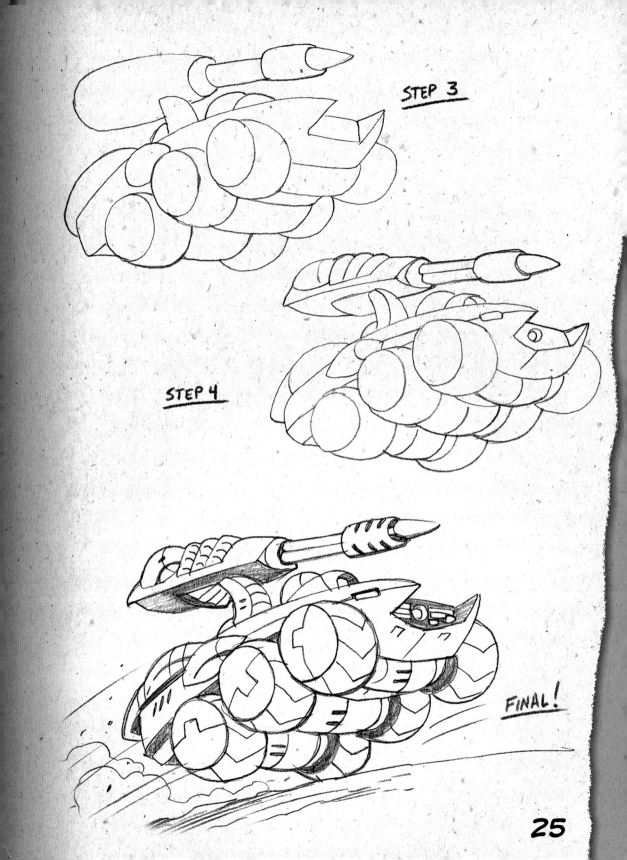

STEP 3

STEP 4

FINAL!

25

B60 Barricade Buster

The B60 Barricade Buster is specially designed to break through any enemy's defenses. Its massive steel ram can burst through concrete barriers and walls up to 2 feet thick. No enemy can hide from this charging beast!

After mastering this drawing, try showing the B60 plowing through an even bigger obstacle!

STEP 1

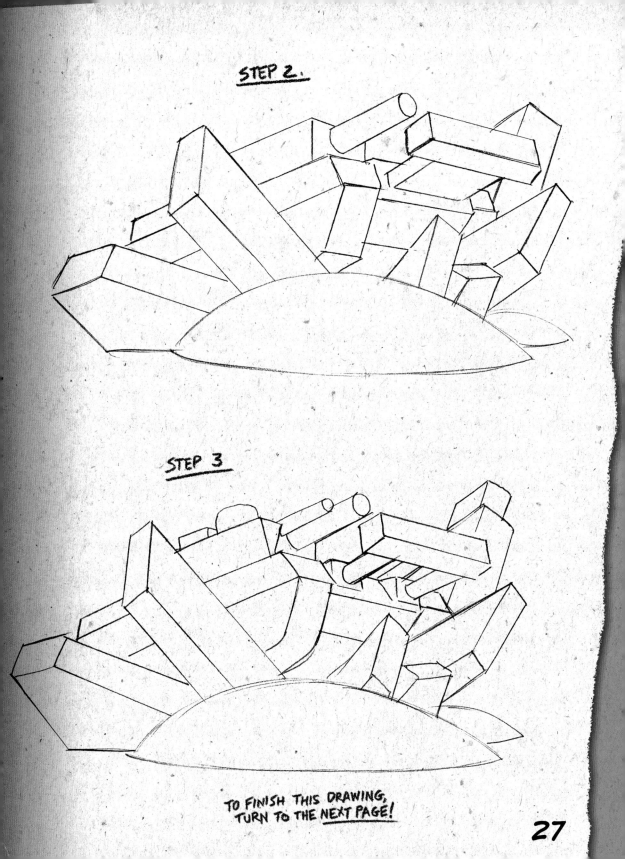

STEP 2.

STEP 3

TO FINISH THIS DRAWING,
TURN TO THE NEXT PAGE!

27

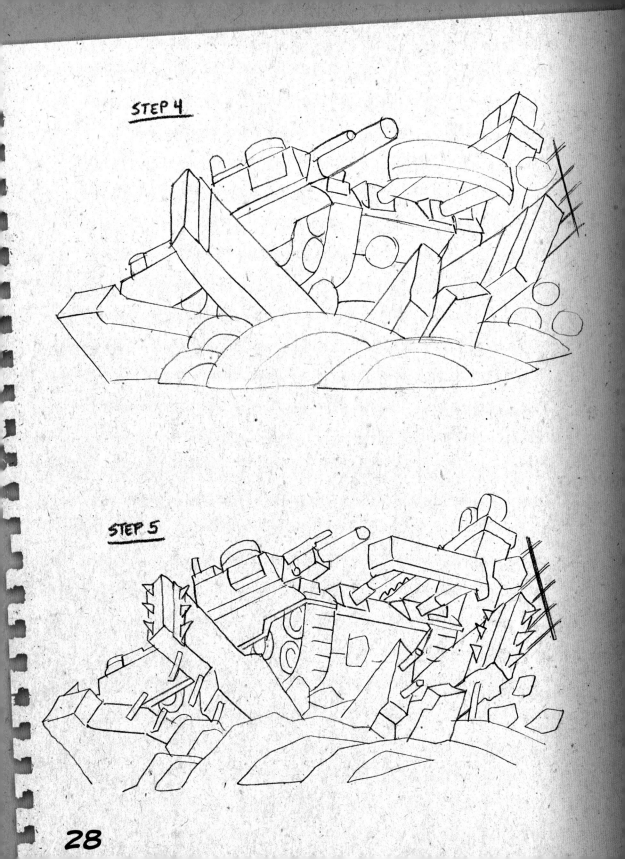

STEP 4

STEP 5

28

STEP 6

FINAL!

GLOSSARY

ammunition (am-yuh-NI-shuhn) — objects fired from guns

barrier (BA-ree-uhr) — a fence or wall that prevents people from entering an area

land mine (LAND MINE) — a bomb that is buried underground

laser (LAY-zur) — a thin, high-energy beam of light

pincer (PIN-sur) — a claw used to grasp and hold objects

plasma (PLAZ-muh) — a highly charged state of matter that is usually formed only inside stars

ravine (ruh-VEEN) — a deep, narrow valley with steep sides

terrain (tuh-RAYN) — land or ground

unique (yoo-NEEK) — one of a kind

READ MORE

Graham, Ian. *Tanks.* The World's Greatest. Chicago: Raintree, 2006.

Parker, Steve. *The M1 Abrams Main Battle Tank.* Cross-Sections. Mankato, Minn.: Capstone Press, 2008.

Parker, Steve. *The M109A6 Paladin.* Cross-Sections. Mankato, Minn.: Capstone Press, 2008.

INTERNET SITES

FactHound offers a safe, fun way to find Internet sites related to this book. All of the sites on FactHound have been researched by our staff.

Here's how:
1. Visit *www.facthound.com*
2. Choose your grade level.
3. Type in this book ID **1429613017** for age-appropriate sites. You may also browse subjects by clicking on letters, or by clicking on pictures and words.
4. Click on the **Fetch It** button.

FactHound will fetch the best sites for you!

INDEX

31901055399739